Wise Words
&
Witty Expressions

by

Reneé Gatz

Woodpecker Press, LLC
Cedar Grove, NJ

Wise Words & Witty Expressions

Copyright © 2009 by Reneé Gatz. All rights reserved.

Woodpecker Press books may be ordered through booksellers or by contacting:
Woodpecker Press, LLC
PO Box 179
Cedar Grove, NJ 07009-0179
www.WoodpeckerPress.com
info@woodpeckerpress.com

ISBN: 978-0-984-15160-8 (sc)
ISBN: 978-0-984-15161-5 (hc)
ISBN: 978-0-984-15162-2 (ebk)

Printed in the United States of America
Hoboken, New Jersey

Cover design: Hit Designs, www.hitdesigns.com
Author photos: Irina Smirnova, www.sigenphotography.com
Photo on p. iii: Gene Lucas Photography, Holmdel, NJ

Dedication

For my parents, Pat and Jack Gatz,
who have provided me with the benefit of their
example, experience, and unconditional love.
I am one lucky girl!

Pat and Jack Gatz

Table of Contents

Reneé and her mom, Pat

Introduction

While growing up as one of three sisters in a traditional Irish-Catholic family, it seemed that for every life experience—big or small—my parents had an expression that could teach me a lesson, remind me what was important, or provide insight into a situation or person. Naturally, as a child I was not yet wise enough to appreciate the value of what was being said to me. I would roll my eyes at my parents and promise myself that I would never repeat these pearls of wisdom.

Well, the joke was on me. I paid far more attention than I realized and, in spite of myself, began using these expressions. Initially, when one would slip out, I would be horrified that I was actually saying something my parents had said to me all too often. I tried to fight it, but it was useless. Apparently, these sayings had affected me more than I knew. Finally, I simply accepted them as part of my vocabulary and began to notice their ability to provide me with clarity when life got confusing—or too big or too small or too hard. There was comfort in knowing I heard these sayings all my life and my parents had heard them throughout their lives, and yet through all these years, they continued to be meaningful, inspiring, funny, and helpful.

I have often been surprised when I would drop one of the expressions captured in this book into conversation that whomever

I was speaking with would begin laughing or would give me that now-I-get-it look or would say "that really helped."

My purpose in writing this book was to share with others the wealth of good common sense that my parent's expressions provided me with. I hope you enjoy reading this collection of expressions and find as much wisdom, value, and humor in them as I have.

Reneé Gatz
August, 2009

Special note to my readers: I've heard these expressions all my life and don't take credit for originating any of them. I believe that they were just handed down generation to generation. If you know other sayings that you'd like to share with me, please visit my blog at www.ReneeGatz.com to post yours or to contact me. Likewise, if you know the source of any of these sayings, I'd like to hear from you as well so I can give credit to whom it is due in my next book and ongoing online collection.

Some of My Favorites!

Let's begin with a few of my favorite expressions so you can get a sense of what you can look forward to as you read *Wise Words & Witty Expressions*. These favorites appear again within their respective chapter, where you will find an explanation or description of each of them.

A good reputation is a very easy thing to lose and a very hard thing to get back.

If only wishing it made it so.

Give me a hit off that pipe you are smoking.

Would you jump in my grave that fast?

The Irish have a way of telling you to go to hell so that you look forward to the trip.

Looks fade, stupid is forever.

Offer it up for the poor souls in purgatory.

Who cares what they think? Are they putting food on your table or paying your bills?

"American" ends in I CAN.

Put your troubles in a bag and drop them over the bridge on your way over here.

Small minds with little to do.

Actions speak louder than words.

People who bring a bone take a bone.

We earned our own, and I would not want to deprive you of the privilege of earning your own.

You can't live with the dead.

Everything happens for a reason.

You can't put an old head on young shoulders.

Don't bring shame to your father's name.

The dead can't hurt you. It's the living you have to worry about.

When you are at the end of your rope, tie a knot and hold on.

There is a little bit of good in the worst of us and a little bit of bad in the best of us.

Loose lips sink ships.

Who do you think you are?

Give me my roses now, not when I am dead.

You don't know a mother's love until she is buried beneath the sod.

Only give your tears to someone who deserves them.

Write it on the ice.

Just because there's snow on the roof does not mean there's no fire within.

Your best days are ahead of you.

You can shut your door on a thief, but there is nothing you can do about a liar.

Anything worth doing at all is worth doing well.

If brains were dynamite, you wouldn't have enough to blow your nose.

Act your age and not your mentality.

Those are the breaks of naval aviation.

It's All about You

We seem to be living in a time when self-responsibility is not a highly sought after ambition. That is most unfortunate because the only person anyone has any control over is themselves. If each person strived to consider how their behavior, or lack thereof, impacted others, society at large, or even themselves, then we could certainly begin to move toward living in a more harmonious world or, at the very least, become happier, more self-fulfilled people. This chapter contains a collection of expressions that may help motivate and remind you of the importance of self-responsibility and where that line begins and where it ends.

It's nice to be important, but it's more important to be nice.

A gentle reminder to mind our manners and be kind.

Get over yourself.

Said to someone who thinks they are a legend in their own mind.

Don't wallow in self-pity.

Pull yourself together and do something positive.

If you are going to dislike someone, you better do it because of something they did to you or someone you love—not because someone else does not like them.

I heard this often growing up. It reminded me to think for myself. And if I was going to use energy to dislike someone, it should be for a good reason.

Do unto others as you would have them do onto you.

If only everyone would follow this golden rule.

Nobody likes a smart aleck, a know-it-all, or a wisenheimer.

Should be obvious.

Self-praise stinks.

Don't be a show-off.

Nobody makes you do anything.

You are responsible for your actions.

Oh what a tangled web we weave, when first we practice to deceive.

It is hard work being a liar. You have to remember all those lies in order not to get caught in them.

Pride cometh before the fall.

There's always somebody bigger and better than you who can put you in your place.

J-E-A-L-O-U-S
Jealousy, jealousy—Didst thou ever offend me? No, not once didst thou knock at my door that I was not ready to attend to thee.

My mother would say this to me in a sing-song voice whenever I would be jealous of my sisters or felt someone was getting more attention than me. It reminded me how ridiculous I was being and that there was no need for jealousy.

You can lead a horse to water, but you can't make it drink.

Unless someone __wants__ to do something, you can't make them.

You burnt your ass, you sit on the blisters.

In other words, if you screw up, you have to own the consequences of your behavior and not expect someone else to take the blame or the burden.

People who live in glass houses should not throw stones.

A reminder that just because you have it a little better than someone else, you should not judge them because you don't understand their experience.

If you don't have anything nice to say, then don't say anything at all.

Keep your mouth shut.

Be a lady (gentleman).

A little decorum is always recommended.

If you knew your prayers as well as you knew that garbage, you'd be a lot better off.

A reminder said to me often as a child when I paid more attention to things that were virtually meaningless rather than to important things like saying my prayers.

If everyone was jumping off the bridge, would you do it too?

A reminder to be a leader. Think about what you want to do and make an intelligent choice.

You can't control other people's behavior—you are only responsible for yours.

Don't fret about how other people act; there is nothing you can do about it. You can, however, control your response to the behavior of others.

Don't get cocky.

It's wrong to act too full of yourself, because it's most unattractive.

That's not nice.

Said to someone whose behavior was less than acceptable.

Don't start something you can't finish.

Know your limitations.

Don't do anything you would be ashamed to tell your parents about.

Behave yourself!

Pray on it.

*When I would ask for my mother's help
with a problem I did not know how to
respond to and it was a decision that only
I could make, she would tell me to pray
about it. By taking the time to pray about
it and with God's help, I would be able to
come to the right conclusion.*

Lead by example.

Doing the right thing can be contagious. When you practice good behavior, others will notice and you will develop credibility among your peers.

A fool and his money are soon parted.

Money deserves respect, and good decisions need to be made to acquire it. If you don't respect it and don't make good decisions, you won't have money for very long.

Anything worth doing at all is worth doing well.

This was a personal favorite of my father's. He had a great talent in woodworking. He always took pride in his work and wanted me to do likewise.

Don't ask someone else to do something you yourself would not do.

A good leader does not ask someone to do something they would not be morally comfortable doing themselves.

Idle hands are the devil's workshop.

Everyone needs a goal to work toward in order to stay engaged in positive energy. If you don't have a goal to work toward, you'll have too much time on your hands and may find negative ways to pass the time.

Remember who you are and where you come from.

I was reminded of this by my mother every time I went on vacation, or out with friends or colleagues. In other words, you can't run from yourself and be someone else simply because you are outside your environment. It also keeps you grounded and less likely to make foolish decisions.

Discretion is the better part of valor.

Sometimes you can exhibit more courage in a given situation by simply exercising discretion.

Start toeing the line.

Said to someone who is not following the rules.

"American" ends in I CAN.

A reminder of our country's spirit.

Weigh your words.

Think before you speak.

Respect your elders.

They deserve it—they have lived through far more than you have.

No sense complaining; no one wants to listen.

A simple rebuke for self-pity.

It doesn't cost anything to be polite.

There's no excuse for not being polite.

Can't means you won't.

A favorite of my mother's when I would give up. She reminded me that it's not that I can't, it's that I am not willing to try harder.

Start carrying your fair share. (Stop watching from the sidelines, get in the game.)

Reminder that you are not participating.

Life's Little Challenges

Sometimes it's the little challenges in life that prevent us from being at peace. Far too often people will try to unload their unrest on others, either knowingly or unknowingly. When this happens, these exchanges can turn an otherwise peaceful state of mind into a full-blown state of aggravation.

At other times, we can be our own source of stress when we consume ourselves with matters over which we have no control and allow ourselves to be consumed with the enormity or tediousness of a situation, the pettiness of another's behavior, or when we may simply dwell on the negative.

The next time you feel life's little challenges beginning to steal away your peaceful state of mind, you may find it helpful to recall one of the expressions captured in this chapter so that you can take back your peace and joy!

Count your blessings.

It's hard to remain unhappy when you are remembering all the things you have to be grateful for.

Be above that. (Don't stoop to their level.)

Just because one person or a group of people behaves badly, doesn't mean you should react in kind. Remember to exhibit behavior that reflects your character and you'll feel a lot better about yourself.

Measure twice, cut once.

My father did beautiful woodworking and always said this when working on a project. It is useful in life too. Evaluate what you are about to do so you get it right the first time.

Mind your own business.

So much aggravation could be avoided if we would just keep this thought in mind.

No worries.

A phrase said after someone apologizes for appearing to have intruded on your time or feelings. This is a reply you'd say to those that sincerely apologize.

Offer it up for the poor souls in purgatory.

The souls in purgatory have it a lot worse than you do, so say a few prayers for them instead of feeling sorry for yourself!

At any rate...

This phrase serves as a great segue to change the subject.

Tomorrow is another day.

A reminder that you always get a second chance.

You need to eat a peck of dirt before you die.

Said to someone who is being a germ-o-phobe.

It will get better.

Keep telling yourself this, and it will.

You will have your day in court. (Every dog has its day.)

You will eventually have your opportunity to be heard or recognized.

The party is over.

The time during which someone has had the ability to take advantage of a situation has ended.

Shit or get off the pot.

Stop procrastinating.

That's neither here nor there.

What you say to someone who is completely off base in a conversation and you need to bring back to the matter at hand.

Just ignore them.

People who like to agitate others are looking for a response from you so they can continue bothering you. It's no fun when you don't give them a reaction to their behavior. Eventually, they get bored and move on to someone else.

Two wrongs don't make a right.

Vengeance will solve nothing. It will, however, create another problem.

A lack of planning on your part does not constitute an emergency on my part.

Said to someone who procrastinated in completing their part of a project and then expects you to make them a priority—with no regard for your schedule.

Especially for Moms

Moms have the world's toughest job. I remember all the little life challenges my sisters and I provided our mother with on a daily, nonstop basis, and she had plenty of expressions to help her keep order and her own sanity.

If I heard the following expressions once, I heard them a thousand times. Many of you may have heard them too. I'd like to dedicate the following expressions to all the mothers navigating their way through a day raising spirited children and to remind them that eventually they grow up and move out!

Don't touch anything.

Promptly said before we entered a store or someone's house.

Don't make me get up.

You really didn't want this to happen. This was your warning that you had pushed it just about as far as she was going to tolerate. Any more would result in uncomfortable consequences.

It is B-E-D time.

Her favorite hour of the day.

Kid, I have been where you are—you
have yet to get where I am.

*Said to me by my mother when I thought
I knew as much or more than she did. I
was quickly corrected with this statement.*

Because I'm the mother. (Because I said so.)

Mothers don't need to explain their logic.

If you would just learn to control that mouth, you would be so much better off.

I heard this expression more times than I can count. My mother was trying to tell me that I can be my own worst enemy when I push the envelope too far.

You'll be sorry.

Another phrase that reminded me that I was on thin ice.

Keep it up and I'll give you something to cry about.

Crying did not work with my mother. Tears did not move her to change her mind. In fact, it just made the situation worse.

You don't know how good you've got it.

When I would complain, I was promptly reminded that I really did not have anything to complain about, considering the life I had compared to some less fortunate people. You know what? I didn't.

1-2-3…

Another telltale sign that she had reached her limit.

If you do something (wrong), you will be better off if you tell me. If I hear about it from someone else, you are really going to be sorry.

Truer words were never spoken. This was her way of saying, "Don't embarrass me in public." It encouraged me to consider my behavior even when she was not looking, because my behavior—good or bad—would reflect on her and our family.

You're trying my patience.

Another reminder that you better reconsider your position or behavior.

I don't want to hear any backchat.

Pretty much that she has spoken and does not want to hear my rebuttal.

Don't test me.

Children have a way of pushing to see how much they can get away with. This was yet another way of saying that you have reached the limit of what you will be allowed to get away with.

I'm not one of your little friends. I'm your mother, and you will speak to me with respect. (I'm not your friend, I am your mother.)

My mother knew I did not need more friends, but did need a parent — and she wanted me to think about the difference. Parents deserve respect from their children. They are committed to us; friends come and go.

That's just the angels bowling in heaven.

Said to children to explain the noise that thunder makes.

I don't care what (so-and-so's) parents said. In this house…

She is the boss and the boss makes her own rules.

Wait until your father gets home.

This was a favorite line after a long day of endless childhood pranks and bad behavior. Of all her lines, this one had the most impact and was reserved for the moment she could take no more. I promise you, at this point, all bad behavior ended and the begging for forgiveness began.

Who do you think you are?

This question was really not meant to be answered. If you did try to answer, well, you would not do it the next time she asked. She was reminding me of my place in the family food chain. In other words, she was the boss, not me.

When you have your own house you can hang your ass out the window for all I care, but as long as you live in my house you will follow my rules. Do you hear me? (Which is really not meant to be answered.)

This is all about respectful behavior and appreciating everything that's been provided for you.

Just wait until we get home.

No good was going to come from this comment. It was too late to make it right, and all warnings were used up. This was her way of telling me that I was in big trouble.

Kid, I have forgotten more than you know.

Yet another reminder that my mother was pretty sharp and not impressed with what a smart aleck I thought I was.

As long as you live under my roof…

Again, this is just a reminder that she sets the house rules.

Look it up in the dictionary.

*I heard this all through my school years.
With my mother there were no shortcuts.
She would not provide me with the
answers. She used to say that if you look
it up, you will remember it.*

I'll turn this car around and we will go home if you kids don't knock it off right now.

Another one of those warning messages.

We can use God's light.

Said to remind me to not turn on the lights in the house unnecessarily.

Those tears don't cut any ice with me.

My mother's way of telling me that crying won't help my situation.

Can't you think of a better way to express yourself? (That's a sign of a poor vocabulary.)

Said to me when I would use slang or worse to express my dissatisfaction with something. In other words, express yourself intelligently.

If you leave this house, you can leave it the same way you came into the world…with nothing.

As a child, I thought foolishly that my threats to run away would get me what I wanted. Well, this statement made me realize that perhaps my parents really do a lot for me that I could not do for myself.

Sleep tight and don't let the bedbugs
bite.

*Said to me as a child each night before I
went to bed, which was proceeded by my
mother making the sign of the cross on
my forehead and saying, "God bless you."*

Think before you open that mouth.

Another one I heard quite a bit. Children don't think about the consequences of their words. I was reminded regularly about this.

Surviving Life's Ups and Downs

Let me state the obvious—no one ever said it was going to be easy to navigate your way through life. All kinds of challenging events present themselves. Some we can see coming, some we create for ourselves, and some we are completely blindsided by. There it is though, staring at us, challenging us, daring us, just plain annoying us, and defying us to manage another new challenge. Don't give up, because what you learn from these experiences makes you a richer and more interesting person. Some of the expressions that follow may be just the motivational weapon you need to win the battle against life's ups and downs or allow you to help someone else win theirs.

When you get knocked down, you pick yourself up, dust yourself off, and start all over again.

Get knocked down seven times, get up an eighth.

What does not kill you makes you stronger.

Appreciate life's challenges.

God helps those who help themselves.

I think this speaks for itself.

Cream always rises to the top.

My parents always told me stories about how the milkman would deliver milk to the front porch very early in the morning. On cold days, the cream (which was the best part) would collect on the top of the milk. This expression is reflective of that, meaning that the best eventually are recognized, even if it takes a while.

Kill them with kindness.

Don't give your detractors anything negative to say about you. It will bother them more if you don't let them know you are upset by their comments or behavior.

If only wishing it made it so.

You can't just make a wish in order for your dreams to come true. You have to take action to help them come to pass.

You can't talk to crazy.

When someone is completely irrational, as much as you would like to work out an amicable solution to a disagreement, you won't have much success. It is best to simply avoid future confrontation.

Don't paint the devil on the door till he's already there.

In other words, don't presume you have trouble until you know it. You could spend a lot of time worrying about something that may never happen.

Pray for yourself too.

Remember to think of yourself in prayer and not just everyone else.

You are not getting paid more whether you do it the easy way (your way) or the hard way (their way). There's no extra pay for the aggravation.

After working in a corporate environment for years and shaking my head and watching others shake their heads at various "strategic" decisions, one begins to realize the truth in this statement. I once said this to a co-worker, and she stopped, looked at me, and said, "You are right, why bother getting aggravated?

If it walks like a duck and quacks like a duck, chances are it's a duck.

Trust your instincts as to what is going on regardless of what others would have you believe.

If God shuts a door, he opens a window.

Be patient and believe that another opportunity will present itself, and it will be even better.

Don't have a defeatist attitude.

Think positive.

Pick yourself up by your bootstraps.

When you get knocked down by life, grab hold and pick yourself up and get back in the game on your own. Don't succumb to failure.

Stand up straight and walk with pride.

Have a positive attitude and appearance.

Who cares what they think? Are they putting food on your table or paying your bills?

Don't let others' opinions weigh on you. Their opinions and comments don't really matter, just yours do.

You come from good stock, you will
be just fine.

When things piled up and I reached a
point of frustration, my mother would
always say these words to remind me that
my ancestors have been through difficult
times and survived—and I will too.

Illegitimati non carborundum est. (Latin translation: Don't let the bastards grind you down!)

Don't let the words of your enemies detract you from your dreams or your peace.

God only gives you what you can bear.

A reminder that you will get past a troubling time, situation, or problem.

Keep your eye on the prize.

Don't allow distractions to cause you to lose sight of your goals.

You can wish in one hand and shit in the other and see which one you have more of.

A reminder to consider the reality of your situation and not just focus on what you wish it was.

Make peace with it.

If something has come your way that won't change, then only you can change.

You don't know what tomorrow will bring. (Tomorrow is another day.)

Something great can be just around the corner. Hang in there to see what it is.

When life hands you lemons, make lemonade.

Make the best of a bad situation.

Put your troubles in a bag and drop them over the bridge on your way over here.

In other words, leave your worries behind and enjoy the moment by not letting those worries prevent you from happiness.

You'll survive to tell the tale.

A reminder that nothing will get the better of you and you will survive to share your experience with someone. This can also be said with sarcasm to someone who is fretting over a trivial issue.

Hard times help build character.

Who wants to hear this during hard times? But it's true. These are the moments that help define the people we will be in the future. They are necessary for our personal growth.

When it rains, it pours—but the sun always comes out again.

When things start to go downhill, look out! But have faith that things will eventually improve.

In God's due time.

*Said to me by my mother to remind me
that God is in control and there are very
good reasons why I need to wait for
whatever I'm wishing for.*

Rise to the occasion.

When a challenge presents itself, take it on and don't walk away.

Wisdom in Life Experience

There's nothing like the "school of hard knocks" to provide you with the "on-the-job" experience required to more easily navigate life's complexities. For example, in your given profession, learning in school is one thing but the practical experience you get from your job is where the real learning and continued learning takes place. The same is true of life. The more life experience we attain, the more we are able to appreciate our experience and the more we can begin to understand the experiences of others, which ultimately can lead to a richer and more fulfilling existence.

Oh, but that on-the-job learning can be painful at times and cause us to easily lose perspective. You may find the following expressions helpful to remember when things get tough and you need to refocus so you can more easily navigate those periods of growing pains.

Your best days are ahead of you.

A positive affirmation for difficult times.

Make hay while the sun shines.

When life presents you with an opportunity take it, don't delay.

Plan your work and work your plan.

My father's high school shop teacher said this to his class, and my father never forgot it. If you think through what you want to do, plan it out, and execute on it, then you have a higher probability of achieving success.

The grass is always greener on the other side.

If someone's life looks rosy on the outside, that does not mean that it's the same behind closed doors. In other words, embrace your life—both the good and the bad.

If you could put down your troubles and pick up someone else's, you would pick your own troubles back up again.

When you look around and say that you wish you had someone else's life, you are also saying that you are willing to give up all the positive attributes of your life. And you would really miss those attributes.

Don't talk about others because you don't know what will come home to roost.

Don't gossip about the goings on in someone else's life because the very thing you're gossiping about could enter your life.

Don't compare yourself to anyone

...because there is only one you.

Birds of feather flock together.

You pick your friends, not your family. People you select to associate with have a direct reflection on your character.

Winners never cheat and cheaters never win.

A simple lesson of morality.

Give the devil his do.

Even though you may disagree with or dislike someone, when they are right or do something well, be big enough to acknowledge it.

Time will tell.

Life doesn't provide immediate answers. Sometimes you have to wait.

You can't take it with you.

Don't allow yourself to become consumed by material things; in the end those "things" are just left behind for someone else's use.

Time heals all wounds.

Things will not seem so bad in retrospect.

You have to crawl before you can walk.

Remember this when life is not meeting your expectations fast enough.

Stick to your guns.

Believe in yourself and do not waiver under pressure—real or perceived.

On New Year's Day, eat pork because a pig roots forward, a chicken scratches back.

Every New Year's Day I heard this expression. It is a positive affirmation to look forward to blessings in the new year and not focus on the past.

What goes around comes around.

Whatever energy or emotion, positive or negative, that you put out, it will come back to you.

Be careful what you wish for—you might just get it.

Sometimes we want and wish for something, and then when it arrives, it's not all that we anticipated and then we wish that we never received it.

You can't put an old head on young shoulders.

It's unfair to expect a young person to have the same wisdom as an older person.

Know your own mind.

Know what is right for you and remain true to that.

Pins and needles, needles and pins, a happy woman is a woman who grins.

Sometimes for the sake of peace, it is best to simply smile and say nothing rather than to provide unwelcome commentary, even if you are right. The trick is having the wisdom to know when and when not to apply this philosophy.

Your chickens have come home to roost.

All the bad decisions you made have now caught up with you.

No one said it was going to be easy.

It's a reminder to see problems through regardless how challenging they may be.

Life's not fair.

Yet another observation and reminder that complaining is not going to change anything.

If you want something bad enough, you'll find a way.

A reminder that you have the imagination and ability to figure out how to get what you want.

Watch the pennies—the dollars will take care of themselves.

It's the number of little expenses that could prevent the accumulation of wealth.

Look before you leap.

Before you start a project, do your research and understand what you are getting into.

Don't judge someone until you have walked a mile in their moccasins.

My parents had an old Indian prayer that included this line. I remember reading it often because it hung over our family's telephone. It served as a reminder not to be judgmental.

Don't do anything where you can't walk down the street with your head held high.

By making smart decisions, you will never need to be ashamed of your actions.

You can get used to hanging if you hang long enough.

People can adapt to anything, given enough time, even if it's painful. Don't get stuck. Make the changes you need to make in order to improve your life.

It's a game of inches.

Life changes don't happen overnight. It's the little successes we have along the way that get us where we want to go. In other words, exercise patience.

Still waters run deep and dark.

A description of why you should not underestimate a very quiet person. They are capable of deep emotional responses to things that appear not to bother them.

Listen more, talk less.

Try to learn from others rather than expound on your opinions.

One of our greatest strengths lies in our ability to laugh at ourselves more than we laugh at others.

Be quicker to see your own mistakes than those of others.

Don't tell tales out of school.

Respect the integrity of your family, friends, and colleagues, and don't share information with others for the express purpose of embarrassing them.

Don't knock your own school.

Be proud of the people and places that made you who you are and don't knock them unfairly or in anger—they represent you, and doing so only degrades you as well.

If it sounds like it's too good to be true, it probably is.

Life does not come easy. If for too little effort something extraordinary is promised, then it's most likely a scam.

Anything worth having is worth working hard for.

A reminder that things that are meaningful are achieved only with great effort. That's what makes them so meaningful.

Not everyone is going to like you.
You need to learn how to deal with
that.

My father told me this when I was very
young and complained about how unfair
a teacher was being to me. He explained
that this will happen throughout my life
and I may as well start getting
comfortable with it.

Fight the good fight.

Fight for the things you feel strongly about. Let the rest go.

Give them enough rope and they will hang themselves.

You don't always have to call someone out. Eventually their own bad behavior will cause them to fail.

The dead can't hurt you. It's the living you have to worry about.

Don't let scary ghost stories bother you. They are just that—stories.

Don't borrow trouble.

Don't create a problem before you actually know if you have one.

Waste not, want not.

Be frugal and reap the rewards.

Cleanliness is next to Godliness.

Strive to be pure in heart, mind, body, and soul.

Judge not lest ye be judged.

Don't be so vocal about others' offenses; we all make mistakes.

See the glass as half-full, not half-empty.

Be optimistic.

No good deed goes unpunished.

Sometimes when you help someone, for some reason it comes back to bite you.

You can catch more bees with a little bit of honey than a whole lot of vinegar.

You can get further with people by behaving with just a little bit of respect rather than a lot of disrespect.

When you are at the end of your rope, tie a knot and hold on.

Encouraging words for when you feel like you can't persevere any longer.

Don't judge a book by its cover.

Not all things are what they seem.

There is a little bit of good in the worst of us and a little bit of bad in the best of us.

No one is perfect—either in a good way or bad.

We earned our own, and I would not want to deprive you of the privilege of earning your own.

If I wanted something, then I had to find a way to earn the money for it. My parents were unapologetic about not giving me whatever I wanted. Of course, I hated this concept as a child, but I am grateful now because I have the ability to be resourceful and truly appreciate what I am able to achieve.

When you lie down with dogs, don't be surprised when you get up with fleas.

If you choose to associate with unsavory characters, then you should not be surprised when you find trouble in your own life.

Don't stay too long at the dance.

Many experiences require you to know when it is best to move on. After a while, you will not be getting out of the experience what you did when you started.

Everything happens for a reason.

Believing this makes life more meaningful.

Sometimes less is more.

The greatest effect can occasionally come from subtlety.

Actions speak louder than words.

Anyone can say anything. Judge someone by what they actually do.

People who bring a bone take a bone.

People who gossip to you about others, gossip to others about you.

Into every life a little rain must fall.

Everyone experiences difficult times. You would not appreciate the good times if you never experienced the bad times.

If you have your health, you have everything.

What is more important in this life?

Money can't buy happiness.

It is an illusion to believe that it can.

An ounce of prevention is worth a pound of cure.

It is easier to prevent a problem than correct one.

Where there's a will, there's a way.

Most things are possible with passion and persistence.

Dream big.

Don't let someone else set limits for you.

It's not what you say, it's how you say it.

Be diplomatic.

Don't bring shame to your father's name.

I was reminded that my father's reputation was stellar—and that I should make sure it stayed that way.

You can do anything you put your mind to.

A reminder that if you want something, you can get it if you apply yourself.

Patience is a virtue.

...and a commendable and beneficial characteristic that provides enduring success and serenity.

Necessity is the mother of invention.

If there is a solution required for something, then that requirement is the seed itself for finding the solution.

Loose lips sink ships.

Don't share information that you expect to remain a secret.

This too shall pass.

The bad times don't last forever.

Walk softly but carry a big stick.

Avoid confrontation but be ready to back up your beliefs.

Cross that bridge when you come to it.

Don't anticipate a problem and try to address it. Wait until you actually have a problem and address it then. You will save yourself a lot of unnecessary grief.

Bloom where you are planted.

Be your best wherever you are. By doing so, you will eventually get to where you want to go.

It's easier to get forgiveness than it is to get permission.

Sometimes, it's best to go for it instead of waiting for everyone to get onboard.

That's life.

It's funny and unpredictable.

Take pride in your appearance.

People will respect you because you are showing them that you respect yourself.

A good reputation is a very easy thing to lose and a very hard thing to get back.

Sometimes all we have is our reputation, so don't throw it away — guard it.

Just be happy you *have* the money to pay the bills.

Said to me by my mother every time I complained about how many expenses I had. Until you don't have a job, you don't realize how fortunate you are to be able to pay the bills, keep your property, and maintain your lifestyle.

That's how angels are made.

An explanation of what can happen if someone behaves in such a reckless manner as to put their life or someone else's life in danger.

Know your audience.

Don't ask for advice from someone who is 180 degrees away from your values. If you do, then don't be surprised when you walk away aggravated.

You meet the same people on the way back down that you met on the way up.

It is important to remain humble and respect everyone that comes into your life, because you will meet the same people in both bad times and good times.

Oh, the Joys and Pains of Love

Love in its infinite variety is the most powerful emotion and therefore provides us with the greatest level of pleasure and the greatest depths of pain. Oh, but it is the spice in life, the stuff that makes everything worthwhile, and the one emotion that transcends death. While it can take us on a wild ride that can temporarily cause us to lose touch with reality or cause us to forget the hard-learned lessons that life has taught us, the following expressions can help you center yourself again so that you can show patience with love or go on to love and laugh again.

If you love someone, set them free. If they return to you, it was meant to be.

An oldie, but a goodie.

Beauty is in the eye of the beholder.

Love makes us see the best in someone.

Give me my roses now, not when I am dead.

Be sure you tell and show the people you love that you love them now; don't wait until it's too late.

How much do I love you? I love you this much (arms outstretched), a bushel and peck, a hug around the neck, a barrel and heap, and I am talking in my sleep about you!

My mother would say this to me in a sing-song voice when I was young and asked her how much she loved me.

There is no accounting for love or taste.

We each have our own values in such things.

Love is blind and marriage is an eye-opener.

When you are in love and dating, you see one side of a person. But once you are married and work your way through life's ups and downs, you get to see a person in their best and worst moments.

You never really know a person until you live with them.

Neither frailties nor strengths are always apparent at first.

You don't know a mother's love until she is buried beneath the sod.

You don't understand the depth of a mother's love until it's taken away from you.

Love others as you would love yourself.

Another golden rule.

You can't live with the dead.

Honor the memory of a loved one by going on to live a happy and fulfilled life.

Nobody loves me and nobody cares. I am going to eat a whole lot of worms and die—big fat juicy ones and itsy-bitsy teensy ones, and I am going to chew them up and spit them in your eye.

My mother would say this to me in a sing-song voice when I was young and feeling sorry for myself and she wanted me to laugh at myself.

There's a lid for every pot.

There exists someone or something right for every person or situation.

It did not work out because something better is meant for you.

Be optimistic (especially after the breakup of a relationship).

Only give your tears to someone who deserves them.

Don't dwell on those who don't appreciate you.

Write it on the ice.

What you say to someone you love, did a favor for, and don't want repayment for. In other words, write the IOU on the ice so it will melt away.

Good looks won't keep the fire burning.

Superficial beauty cannot ensure a lasting relationship.

Just because there's snow on the roof does not mean there's no fire within.

Age doesn't define a person's desire for passion.

Looks fade, stupid is forever.

Pick a mate for more than superficial reasons.

If love fell on horseshit, it would stick.

In other words, there is no accounting for why or who someone will fall for.

Love overlooks a lot.

Amen.

Buzz Off, You're Bothering Me

There's always someone, no matter where you go—work, home, an event, the grocery store, wherever—who wants to bother you or whose existence simply bothers you. They either don't know they are driving you crazy or simply don't care that they are. They can be sneaky, self-serving, untrustworthy, or just plain annoying.

The following expressions can provide you with the mental ammunition you need to keep their shenanigans from having a negative impact on you or can provide you with some snappy repartees to help set the person straight and send them on their way.

She is too sweet to be wholesome.

I can't tell you how many times this expression has proved to be true. If someone is working too hard at being nice to you or is sickeningly sweet, it is usually because they are hiding an ulterior motive and should not be trusted.

You can shut your door on a thief, but there is nothing you can do about a liar.

You can protect yourself from a robber, but it's harder to identify a liar.

Locks keep honest people out. If a thief wants to get in, he will find a way.

I learned this one from my father. I asked him one day why he was putting a lock on our shed. When he said this, I did not understand. He explained that it was a protective measure he was taking, but if someone really wants to steal from you, they will. You have to be prepared for that situation as well.

If they are talking about you, they are leaving someone else alone.

In other words, people are always talking about someone. If today they are talking about you, somebody else is catching a break. Don't focus on what people say in gossip.

She knows more than her prayers.

She is not as innocent as she would have you believe.

They are more to be pitied than to be laughed at.

When someone behaves in an idiotic manner, laughing at the outrageousness of their behavior is less warranted than your pity for their inability to know how to better behave.

They can talk about you all they want, but they can't talk another hole in your ass.

People can talk about you, but all that talk can never change who you really are.

Money talks, bullshit walks.

Another way to say that if someone believes so much in something, they should show some good faith by making a personal investment. If a person is unwilling to do so, then it's best that you walk away.

Empty barrels make the most noise.

People who have the least to contribute often can have the most to say. My mother learned this expression from the nuns that taught her at the all-girl Catholic high school she attended. The nuns used this expression to describe someone who was empty of intelligence and, therefore, when they spoke all they contributed to the discussion was a lot of noise. They, like empty barrels that are jostled, just make a lot of noise.

Consider the source.

When giving weight to someone's words, consider the level of respect you have for the person expressing their opinion.

Put up or shut up.

If someone is going to try to sway others to their opinion, they should only acquire credibility by putting some of their own skin in the game.

Thou dost protest too much.

If someone says too many times that they don't care, then chances are they are trying very hard to cover up how much they really do care.

Small minds with little to do.

An expression that describes people who enjoy trying to hurt others with their gossip.

Suffer in silence.

No one wants to hear anyone complain.

You better shape up or ship out.

Do your part or leave.

The Irish have a way of telling you to go to hell so that you look forward to the trip.

No need to be nasty. If you are creative enough, you can shake off an annoying person. For example, the next time someone asks you out of pure nosiness where you are going, tell them "to hell" if you don't change your ways.

You can't pull the wool over my eyes.

An expression used to call out someone who is trying to fool you.

Don't suffer from fools.

Don't allow someone to convince you of anything or take advantage of your good nature. Recognize insincerity when you see it and take precautions.

He's a wolf in sheep's clothing.

Just because someone seems good does not mean that he is a well-intended person.

Simply Sarcastic

Sometimes the most effective way to make your point is through sarcasm. When done well, sarcasm can break tension, bring a fresh awareness to a situation, or even make someone laugh. It can also throw a person a bit off their game, which may be just the right approach to bring clarity and focus back to a situation that may be getting out of hand. This chapter contains a collection of some snappy statements that you may find helpful when you need to set someone straight or regain control of a situation.

Is that wood I smell burning?

Said when you can tell someone is finally applying themselves.

Use your head for something besides a hat rack.

Think!

You're as handy as a zipper on a doorknob.

Your resourcefulness is doubtful.

Take your drama to your momma.

Please, cut the histrionics.

I don't chew my own cud twice.

This is a crazy one my mother used to say. It meant that she was not going to repeat herself. This is how I learned what cud meant. (Look it up if you don't know what it means.)

Now you're cooking with gas on the back burner.

In other words, you are really getting things done now.

Would you jump in my grave that fast?

A response said to someone attempting to mimic your efforts for their own benefit.

If brains were dynamite, you wouldn't have enough to blow your nose.

You're behavior is irrational and totally illogical.

He/she is a beaut, or a tool, or a piece of work.

Referring to a person who is rather challenging to work with.

Act your age and not your mentality.

This is a whimsical reference implying illogical behavior.

I was born at night, not last night. (Do I look like I was born yesterday?)

In response to someone trying to put one over on you.

Do you know where you can find sympathy?

Answer: Between shit and sweat in the dictionary (where you will not find it either…just like you will not find sympathy here).

Take a powder. (Go pound salt. Hit the bricks. Get lost. Take a hike.)

I haven't the patience for your silly behavior. Leave me alone.

Give me a hit off that pipe you are smoking.

In other words, based on what you said, you must be high because you are talking crazy.

What does that have to do with the price of tea in China?

In other words, your comments do not reflect the current situation—stay on topic or don't speak.

You better shape up or you will find yourself on the outside looking in.

A reminder to behave oneself.

Those are the breaks of naval aviation.

Stuff happens.

You just worry about yourself.

A response said to someone who is too caught up in your business.

Do you kiss your mother with that mouth?

Said to shame a person who uses vulgar language.

Yeah, well you've got another think coming.

Said to someone who "thinks" they have convinced you of something. They may have to rethink it.

Wise up, buff up, or shape up.

Expressions that tell you that you need to improve your behavior.

You are like a bull in a china shop.

Describes a person who is not very delicate.

I am going to go wherever the wind blows me.

Said to someone who is being nosy about where you are going.

You're not sugar; you won't melt in the rain.

Said to someone complaining about going out in inclement weather.

Who died and left you boss?

Said to someone who is taking undue liberties in trying to take control over a situation or person.

I am going to take off for parts unknown.

This is a heads-up to someone getting on your nerves and that you are leaving.

They have more money than they
have sense.

*Used to clarify that just because someone
has a lot of money doesn't mean that they
are very smart.*

Keep it up and I will knock you into the middle of next week.

This is an effective and forceful expression for someone who is getting on your nerves.

Your taste is in your mouth.

You have no sense of style.

Final Thoughts

Throughout the pages in this book, I hope you were inspired, enlightened, and entertained by this collection of "Wise Words & Witty Expressions."

I've enjoyed recalling them and had many laughs remembering the fond memories attached to each of these expressions. It's also been a privilege to honor my family's strength of character and good humor, while acknowledging in a special way my heritage by including the Irish harp throughout the book.

I would very much enjoy learning the expressions that you grew up hearing or are reflective of your cultural background, whether your expressions are based on the region of the U.S. you grew up in or are reflective of your ancestry.

Please visit me at my blogsite www.ReneeGatz.com to share your "Wise Words & Witty Expressions" and let me know if any of these had an affect on you and why. I look forward to hearing from you.

All of life's best to you always!

Index of Expressions
in Alphabetical Order

112

J

K

113

L

M

N

O

P

R

S

117

118

Reneé Gatz

About the Author

Reneé Gatz was born and raised in New Jersey, the oldest of three girls and had always been taken by the strength of character and conviction that her parents displayed. They navigated through life by holding true to their core beliefs. Those beliefs were most often exhibited by their example but were also exhibited in the expressions they used to keep life in perspective, to remind themselves of what was important, and to laugh at foolishness so as not to take life too seriously.

In her early growing years, Gatz did not appreciate the power of the expressions her parents spoke, but as she grew she was amazed at how these expressions would come back to her to provide clarity, understanding, or a laugh at just the right moment.

Many of the expressions she learned growing up were passed on to her through her mother, who learned them from her mother. Gatz's grandmother was a woman of strength and good humor who immigrated alone at the age of 18 to the United States from Ireland in the steerage section of a ship that landed at Ellis Island.

Gatz's late father was a man of few words who relied more on the power of his actions to express himself. Nonetheless, he is credited with teaching Gatz some important life lessons through the use of expression and some sarcastic repartee as well.

Gatz was motivated to share these expressions based on the positive response she would receive when she would mention one in conversation, the surprise that an expression she had heard her entire life was new to someone, and her natural desire to communicate these great thoughts to others.

Reneé Gatz earned her BS in business management from St. Peter's College. She has held a variety of marketing and communications positions in the financial services industry for over fifteen years. She has always enjoyed writing and was inspired to share the wisdom she learned from her parents in this book, *Wise Words & Witty Expressions*. Gatz lives in New Jersey today, not far from her childhood home. To learn more about Reneé Gatz and her book, visit www.ReneeGatz.com.